Amongst the Trembling Apes

Jarrad Ackert

"Man is born in labor:
and there's a risk of death in being born.
The very first things he learns
are pain and anguish: from the first
his mother and father
console him for being born.
Then as he grows
they both support him, go on
trying, with words and actions,
to give him heart,
console him merely for being human:
there's nothing kinder
a parent can do for a child.
Yet why bring one who needs
such comforting to life,
and then keep him alive?
If life is a misfortune,
why grant us such strength?
Such is the human condition,
inviolate Moon.
But you who are not mortal,
care little, maybe, for my words."

- Giacomo Leopardi, Night Song of a Wandering Shepard in Asia

Each and every day is the payment of a debt, the debt of being alive. Time, that pact between meat and perception – the horror of which only man can experience – wears everything out into monotony, vanity, futility; we take on this unceasing burden, this cost, without rhyme nor reason. The continuation of sentient life is the continuation of senseless suffering.

○

To think that millions of men have strived to find their place in the cosmos…and then to damn it all to comedy! to unnecessary strife!

○

While myriads of species send their youth into the chaotic "wild," the human-animal nurtures and advocates for itself, through the offspring, for years on end. As one doctrine of slavery begins as another ends, the eighteen-year old animal is sent into a Hegelian world, molded and shaped for an alleged comfort and pleasure. A deficient species? well, could it be any more obvious?

○

This new notebook in which I write has, in no time, split at the binding. Humanity can do nothing better than produce junk; the species has no confidence in itself beyond the bottom-line.

○

The bullet, the Bible, or the bottle.

○

Obsession is an indication of consciousness.

What am I but a death-wish? What have I ever been but my mind? Do the two not closely correspond to one another? A mind that lives out life in place of a man will gradually fall upon its own insignificance. If I trace back through my obsessions, what else will I find but a non-existent life? : drinking, smoking, Buddhism, antinatalism, Job, Ecclesiastes; solitude, music; fascinations with monasticism, asceticism, hermits and hobos; dreams and perversions; standing on bridges, watching life go by; and at last the thirst for silence; unmatched, defiant silence.

The wisdom of Silenus; Ecclesiastes; Job; the Buddha's four truths; the retreat of Laotse; the sorrow of Heraclitus – there are indeed some bits of wisdom in the oldest of texts. Man seems to have understood his footing quite quickly, and has worked himself for thousands of years to try and forget about it.

Are there any bacteria or viral beings that destroy or manipulate their environment to the drastic consequence of destroying themselves, or this the human-animal alone in that regard? Could it be that chance "life-atoms" acted in such a way eons ago, and we are simply the latest instance of such a catastrophe?

The fate of consciousness is the prolongation of life under guises of possibility and actuality; that is, of belief.

○

Optimism, that blind or forced ignorance of the suffering inherent in animal sentience, must be recognized as emotional immaturity, or simple jackassery.

○

The act of paying rent for some resemblance of quietude relies on one playing the part of a disheveled man from off the street, resigning himself to every willed imprisonment caused by the opportunistic employer.

○

Why is it that some people come to me to vent the airs of their troubles, their griefs, upon my trembling ear? I shudder at the thought of their breath, their words, as much as I do over the thought that I can provide some sort of answer, a way out, for them. What do I have to offer? Why should I have to give anyone anything? I am nothing but an ear; an ear that grows tired of the unmusicality of most men.

○

The advantage of the Desert Fathers and Mothers lies solely in them having been able to air their joy and despair to no contrary but the silence of God.

○

I ask you, how does rumination differ from meditation?

○

Rather my eyes lifted up or down– to the heavens or to the grave; never towards the face of man.

Time is the pact between matter and perception; the horrors of time come from knowing that we are its sole inheritor.

○

The only miracle of this human instance of Biology – and it's consciousness – is its ability to deny itself: asceticism, hermitry, veganism/vegetarianism, celibacy, antinatalism and suicide.

○

In braving the mad world, I find consolation by uttering the following: "no matter what the circumstance, you can always return to your room, alone."

○

It is time to consider all biological "adaptation" (species and traits alike) as biological "outbreak." Every species across all of the so-called kingdoms perpetuate themselves without rhyme nor reason, dominating, or being dominated by, other species to spread across the surface (planet) like contagion. Life, in all its instances, cannot contain itself; it has no bounds but that provided by reduction or extinction. Life is a virus that chokes planets until it can no longer do so. If you are anti-life, consider yourself pro-planet; the most wonderful sound to your ears is that of a dormant cosmos.

○

To become aware of one's blinking; to understand the mechanistic function of this programming…the biological puppet…slave of genetics…the blind drive of indifference…

o

Listen to them as they weep, knowing that they are enslaved by a system and by those of material wealth. Listen and weep for them, for they know not of how deeply rooted their slavery is! The shackles of work, monotony and time; further, the shackle of procreation; and further still: sentience!

o

There is no such thing as equality in biological life; if there was, all specimens would be self-maintaining systems, never knowing of thirst, hunger and cold. Add consciousness to a species and does it ever rear its ugly head! The construct of "race" proves to be a shining example. No, there is no equality in life. Death, that zero-sum of non-existence, however, this is what levels the playing-field. An activist shouts from the soap-box about equality? take care to whisper into their ear, "*never bear a child.*"

o

I am a failure of a "man." The beliefs and codes – pillars which keep this manic structure afloat – have been smashed; the damage is done. I, however, remain in suffering from obsessions, perversions and depressions – including the desire to watch the structure collapse *on everyone.*

o

Spending my evenings downing one beer and whisky after another, I've begun to pass out early and rise in the middle of the night. I think of the ascetics who never permitted themselves much sleep. Alas, I will never attain to their heights: they needed nothing to forget about themselves.

○

Each night, unable to attain a thorough sleep, I anxiously check the clock and hope for the long hours to finally draw to a close. The worst awakening is the first one; from out of the night's drunken stupor, where sleep is akin to death – a state in which no man deserves to be shaken from.

○

Born into the fever of a lie, we abandon that for a convenient dream.

○

Clothing, making man the only animal horrified of itself.

○

Sometimes, a man lies down in a drunken alley; other times, he cracks apart in the rust of old form.

○

The idea that the human species is a moral or evolutionary failure; the debate on whether or not birth control should be permitted – these two vain arguments signal to me that the species has thought too highly of itself; that our time is long past due…

○

One need only look at a building slowly being consumed by vines to realize that all strife is for naught.

o

To anyone inquiring into my stance on any of the multitudinous anthropocentric concerns, I should like to respond with "I have *less important* matters to consider."

o

A small donation made to the impoverished Haredi Jews – I will support any man rejecting the common lot and common dollar for devotion to an interior life.

o

How many gallons of saliva I would have lost, if the old Russian custom of spitting on the floor (upon hearing something distasteful) was still in vogue.

o

My only desire is to die; unlike the rest of the myriad of man's desires, it is the only one to be fulfilled.

o

What we call "health" is but the space between sickness and decay. Real health only arrives through non-existence, when the body is cast away into dust.

○

I wear a Saint Christopher medallion around my neck, having come into it from successive generations. I take it up as a vow: to have this neck be the last that it hangs from.

○

The first bird-song of spring push upon the closed windows. I shudder at the thought of the coming Dionysian circus, that carnival of sex. Terror at the thought of convulsing, electric bodies consuming one another; the ghastly shriek of orgasm…

Lock me up in a monastery bereft of symbology. Or better yet, a simple cell of four white walls. I will gladly wear the chastity belt and swallow the key.

○

One can only hope that these self-imploding societies - puffed-up with chemicals, drugs and fumes – societies of technotropic hallucination, couches, recliners, tight clothing – will cut the grip of nature with blades of infertility and sterility.

○

All beliefs, all ideals, are simply a matter of convenience.

○

I long for eternal possibility in a world of restriction.

○

Emotion makes a schizophrenic out of everyone.

○

I am not here to engage in life, but to comment on it whimsically; waiting until the Great Whatever blows out this candle.

○

Everywhere man sets traps for himself: walk down a sidewalk and realize that you're stepping along a buried gas line. Only a Hegel could be proud.

○

Shameful, that a Christianity was to spread like plague, rather than a Jainism. Yet I suppose that the Indian practice is *too sane* for man, anyways.

○

Seen with an eye looking westward, the reincarnation-cycles of the Jains, Hindus and Buddhists seem like folk-magic; with a slight glance towards the East however, we realize this system was used as a tool of fear towards the initiates: if nothing was more wicked and insufferable than birth and death, simply imagine if the wheel could never be stopped from turning once more, infinitely…

○

For the optimists? God. For the defeatists? Fleeting luck, blind chance.

○

Yes, the Will-to-live is inherent in all things; just listen to the mice pushing themselves under the floorboards.

Writings, idols, monuments and structures – vehicles of our unnecessary propagation.

○

Some prisoners take up the Bible; for others, the pen. I have taken the latter, and not by choice.

○

Rather side with the librarian than the teacher, writer or scholar – the latter *force* opinion, the former coolly *logs* it.

○

The Jewish school in which I work was once a hospital. In the past, people groaned unto their death. Now, it houses those who pray for salvation, in this life or the next. Really, the place has never changed hands.

○

Every word uttered is violence towards silence, a severance with our irrationality.

○

Digestion gives me something to do in afternoons freed from work.

○

I keep my eyes to the carpet; dare not I look through the windows, at the daylight that unsettles most of life.

○

Pulling the shirt away from my scant chest – I'd rather not feel the reverberations of a living pulse.

○

If only flatulence and sighs were the most physical of my exertions!

○

Memory does not unfold unto knowledge – have a look at monotony, will you?

○

"What's going on? Same old?" I ask a student of whose building I clean. He turns to me and states "Same old dirty boots." If only he knew what a revelation that was!

○

I thank the day for its dusk; the convulsions of a night's sleep do me better than the rationality of the sun.

○

Nothing is ever satisfied, ever finished, until the cool fingers of death press tenderly into your shoulders.

○

Recalling a recent moment when I had to use a calculator – I had utterly forgotten how old I was. If that is not a testament to my disinterest in life; a testament to the yawn of ancient cosmic tiredness…

○

As long as it is alive it wants, needs, thrives, decays and dies – and the end is as void as the before.

○

I do not know what keeps me from jumping off of a bridge or running towards the wild, except mere convenience.

○

Not a difference between nature-romanticism and urban-defeatism – both attitudes reflect our discomfort, disarray, and inclination towards necessary illusion.

o

If I had been born in a culture of nature-worship, I would have paid my respects to Autumn only: the chilled air, the heavy, pervading rains, the glacial eyes of the stars, the decay…

o

In my late teenage years, I came to the conclusion that to live until one is twenty-five is more than enough – the length of time having afforded one with all that life has and is. Here I am at that age; it seems as if I had foreseen just how tired I would be at this very moment.

o

An unfortunate sense of optimism arises when we believe that the forthcoming climate disaster can be reversed. Have we any evidence towards such a belief? If we did, would the evidence come from a past event estimated similar in breadth? Granted, we have "documentation" that famine, disease and incredible shifts in geological-meteorological "stability" have occurred, in which certain populations met certain fate. Yet none have occurred for this species zero-sum; at least, none backed by remnants of archeology, paleopathology and culture. If they have, they have yet to be discovered or have disappeared altogether.

   What we are likely to experience first-hand is the extinguishing of the virus that is ourselves. Nature will wash its indifferent hands clean of another of its irrational outbreaks. It is worth noting in a few sentences and in the screams of our unmaking, nothing more.

o

The fifth horseman? Apathy.

○

This one reads The Prince with a feeling of inferiority; that one reads it with an inclination towards superiority: two neuroses that have generated a plethora of sickened parasites. I balk at the idea of power and lament that the species was not able to live up to its fate – as a conscious insignificance.

○

Imprisoned by chemical-release and blind procreation, sex appears as the natural, desirable thing to do. To a mind, aware of its own fiction and enslavement, however, sex is transfigured into a disaster, an abomination. Paralyzed and consequentially celibate is the one who sees the act as a revolting trembling of bodies, sharing in the wealth of a myth – the myth of being someone, something outside of the meaningless mechanics of biological function. Even more disastrous are the horrors of reproduction – propagation of the void's bastards; additional scar tissue of the Absolute (suffering).

I will remain paralyzed, a failure of flesh.

○

Not in favor for the end of sentient life; rather, for the curtain to be drawn on all physical matter.

○

The school's cook has sat in his corner for ten years, watching the arms of the clock sling 'round and 'round in a circle, never going any faster or slower. He prepares three meals a day and in between he sits and waits. Sadness overcomes me, when I see him through the window or enter the kitchen. Yet I know he is an example for mankind. I, the janitor and he the cook – brothers in futility.

○

By being alive, we bear the mark of Koheletic debt – the fruitless vanity and futility of chasing ghosts in a world in which nothing is finished, a world void of rest…

○

…dumb apes, lost in a dream well-tailored to their need for justification and worth…

○

Living in fear of God, he takes it so far as to despair of being at once imprisoned, possessed and infatuated with His omnipresence, His creation.

○

All religions were made for the individual, to join in communal self-loss and solitude; all religions were made for the community, to believe that they were individuals.

○

Consciousness will turn in on itself, always – look at how devotion when from a *state of being* to a rash religious, psychological *term*.

○

How much more Stoic we could have been if each of us, in our youth, had someone with the guts to explain the *actual* nature of man and his exploitations.

○

The animals live amongst us, and we are just as clueless.

○

History? a chronicle of disaster stemming from our own creation – tools, symbols and the yapping mouth.

○

If I were a mathematician and biologist, I would expound a thesis combining stability theory and evolution-as-error: life, existence, etc. is an error; the only chance for this error to become stable would be for the two poles of life and death equalizing out. Since there is ever-more life coming to the surface (planet), the error will inevitably become unstable; the first multiplying-consuming cells were to start it, the virus *homo-sapien* will end it.

○

There is some solace in being up hours before daybreak. Knowing that *they* are still out *there*, yet their eyes are closed…lost in a dream deeper than the one they consciously live in.

○

If consciousness is "sight," how poorly adapted we are as "seers!" Our vision is interpretation – mythological, symbolical, dream-like; an unfortunate tint.

○

Man hid in the caves, terrified of the physical realm; yet no cave was deeper, blacker, warmer than the cave of dreams. The mind? – a beaver's teeth, a butterfly's camouflage; our defense against the Predator.

o

The original despair: a fear-full scream answered only by its own echo.

o

The womb splinters open, spilling out liquid secretion, red throbbing flesh, pain. For months, cellular composition was building upon itself – now the product lies in front of us - blind and screaming. Pushed out like defecation from one prison into another far more binding and sensory, we bow our heads and say: "having made it this far, it deserves to join in the ranks of suffering."

o

Love, a height which is taken to be the end-all of yearning, sinks into tolerance – that valley of futility. Two victims of chemicals and tinted vision; erroneous eyes taking the idea of Self missionary-style.

o

"If life was but a chronicle of laying out the bedsheets for sleep…"

o

When you peel back all of your emotional and mental layers, you really don't know *what* you are.

○

I see some semblance of blood in my father's grandfather, a man who drank and wandered aimlessly only to return to his wife, beating and impregnating her time after time. Great is my own thirst and anger; so I have set myself to drinking in an empty room – a small victory against wicked genes.

○

Consciousness needed to maintain itself as much as a heart needed to beat. So develops the ego, a defense against the horrors stemming from awareness – and the damning creation of meaning. Naturally, we have never looked back.

○

A species that does not see destruction intertwined with its expansion – a species at odds with itself.

○

As a child, I would strangle myself while lying on the couch. Had I known then what fate would have brought me now, I'd have sought the act through.

○

Sadistic medicine men, doctors and psychologists prolong and encourage aging, thinking that they are doing mankind a service… and how right they are! The prolongation of suffering, sickness, decay! A masochistic society's dream has come to fruition in sterile white rooms and leather couches.

How I envy those tombstones of the "too soon."

○

Those days when one would like to be someone else; someone with a plan, a penchant for action. Alas, you come back down from the heights of dreams to waddle through the mud, looking for a soft, low spot to curl back up into.

○

Capitalists, socialists, monarchists and anarchists – rest your heavy hearts! Your theories, systems and lifestyles will simply not stand up to the millions of years it took for cruelty, greed and deception to evolve as adequate traits, suitable for species-reproduction.

○

I would have admired Columbus if his journey was Koheletic – that is, if in search of a New World founded on Divine Intervention he had lost his way, turned back and upon docking at home, reported "ah, nothing new!"

○

To a fault, we far too often look in the mirror or into someone else's eyes and do not recognize a corpse.

○

Life is death reverberating the air.

○

Philosophy began and ended with the ancients – they posed all of the problems that arise from our type of consciousness. Being in a limited framework of abstraction, language and logic-games, we can progress no further, can say no more than they did. What has been termed philosophy since their speculations are nothing but various coping-mechanisms concerning the madness of civilization and culture; more recently, the simulacrum society.

○

I offer nothing to the species but an isolated workplace and the locked room in which I dwell.

○

If anything, remember me as a dreamer: one who accepted his cell and made fruit from conscious romanticization.

○

Housemaids and monks…how I relate these sad cases: inert, bored and cut off from the world; left to face the daily violence of an inner life driven towards its own wall…

○

As far as writers, the void appeals only to those who have gone *beyond* their own death.

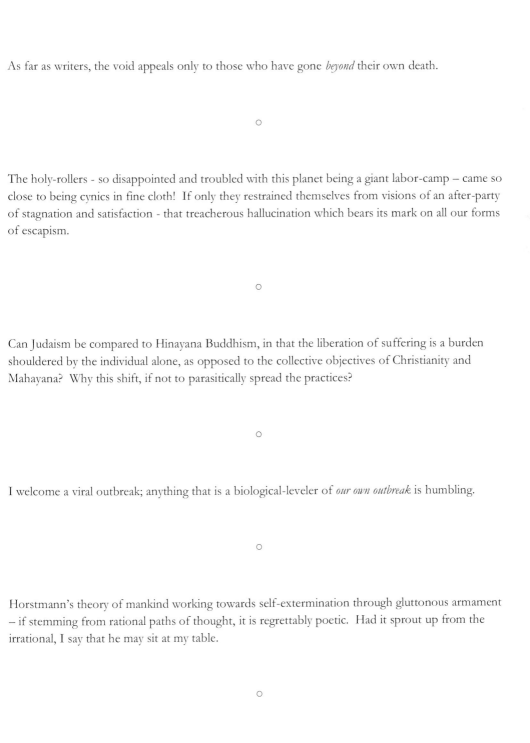

○

The holy-rollers - so disappointed and troubled with this planet being a giant labor-camp – came so close to being cynics in fine cloth! If only they restrained themselves from visions of an after-party of stagnation and satisfaction - that treacherous hallucination which bears its mark on all our forms of escapism.

○

Can Judaism be compared to Hinayana Buddhism, in that the liberation of suffering is a burden shouldered by the individual alone, as opposed to the collective objectives of Christianity and Mahayana? Why this shift, if not to parasitically spread the practices?

○

I welcome a viral outbreak; anything that is a biological-leveler of *our own outbreak* is humbling.

○

Horstmann's theory of mankind working towards self-extermination through gluttonous armament – if stemming from rational paths of thought, it is regrettably poetic. Had it sprout up from the irrational, I say that he may sit at my table.

○

"We pay our dues and the Lord will compensate!" has been replaced with "we pay with our life and we *will* feel *good* about it!" A fresh coat of paint on an old, dilapidated wall.

○

One in a million, as the saying goes, that I came to birth by a chance egg and chance sperm. And so I envy the 999,999.

○

We who deny the Will-to-live shall crawl into a corner for the sake of all of sentient existence – that killing-field, slaughterhouse and feeding-trough we call "physical matter."

○

Vapid afternoons spent lying about the bedroom, thinking that what would be best for me would be to shut both the closet and entrance doors, only to open them and find two closets.

○

I look out the window and laugh at the apes-on-wheels.

○

Here at the age of twenty-five, my father admits for the first time that he was married to another woman before my mother. Had one turn of fate never came about, I'd have been spared from existence! A comedic solace to define the rest of my life by.

○

Judaism preaches marriage, for without a wife one is only "half a person." What gymnastics of logic it must take to tip-toe around the irrational drive of procreation and to affirm the false Order man so desperately craves.

○

The paradox of despising consciousness, yet devoting oneself to an interior life…

○

If there ever was a time in which man did not try to know anything, surely this was the period spent in the Garden.

The Judaic Shabbat is the vision of a return to this paradise we so longingly yearn for. The cessation of action; the end of our collective koholetic debt; fruits born without our labor, pain and grief – no longer needing, much less needing to *know* anything.

The Shabbat is to the Jewish what Nirvana is to the Buddhist. Yet take it further – have courage, men! Put desire into our biological extinction: this we need not dream up, mythologize.

What began in a dream can end in collective asceticism, celibacy, birth control and suicide: to live as though dead, or to join the dead immediately.

○

This rabbi, when I ask him if it's enjoyable to have an entire floor of dormitories to himself, replies as I would had I been in his situation: "Some people think it's bad to not have company."

Surely, this man abides by his own temperament before his Law. Again: "Even if I were to go and visit my parents for the holiday, I'd still be on the computer all day; so what's the difference?"

Here is a man who risks being ostracized by his community for the peace of four walls and his own mind. And so the community has but *one* man.

○

Notes of monetary debt arrive in the mail. The calendar represents a countdown to the consequences of having acted, of simply being alive. Endless strife and hunger not being payment enough, we earn the shuffling of debts and papers, blowing kisses to each other for this collective misery.

○

If it is all pre-destined? - to hell with the creator. If it is a miracle? - well, nothing should have come about ; not even a *silent universe* is worth surpassing *nothing*.

○

A man with an affinity for solitude is worth knowing – at his discretion.

○

Knowing that fate possesses your every atom, how should one get through life? Possess little to call your own, abandon hope, and prepare for any and every form of disaster.

○

Air-conditioning controls chaos.

○

I tried transgressing norms and that only led to terror. And that terror led to a deeper one, the most primordial of all: terror of *myself.*

○

Nobody sleeps in the ghettos.

○

"You'd end up being bored if you didn't work." Find me somebody who isn't bored ad infinitum and I'll make sure to record the being as something *beyond sentience.*

○

I feel tired; it's an exhaustion that no amount of sleep could cure. If I were to drink an entire pot of coffee, it would be merely for the sake of whiling away the hours. This tiredness penetrates through all things – I sense the ancient silence of the cosmos. On this planet, the whirling of the seasons is no more than a prolonged sigh. In me, consciousness grows weary. The triad of monotony, futility and vanity stand as the last remaining symbol for my being to identify with; eventually this too shall lie down in the graveyard

○

If, one day, I refuse to pay taxes, it's only because I will be content with a cell provided, food prepared, Eden revealed.

○

A tractatus:

1. Physical matter is something that should never have been.
2. One should never give birth.
3. Extinction of all matter is vital to quietude, the state of nirvana.

○

Being locked inside of four walls, one experiences the weaving of stagnation and transience within the solitary. The ennui of being alone, the welling-up of dreams and obsessions: the mind watching itself eventually looks about the room, at the objects, the walls – and perceives ruin. Everything around us and our own person – subjects of entropy. Everything is a prop to be demolished in the workings of fate.

History and time – two poorly conceived concepts. The rapid consumption and destruction of man's workings (symbols, myths, bellies, ovaries and sperm) proves our viral nature: an outbreak of the irrationally perceived infinite; outright ignorance of temporality and anthropomorphic insignificance.

If we have failed to look at physical existence on the whole as its own destroyer; if we continue to believe in mythologies; if we remain non-skeptical of "natural reproduction" as the basis for our fear and confusion – we will pay the debt nevertheless: in confusion for some, liberation for others.

○

My writings? - merely annotations of destruction through creation; comments on a magnificent error, a grandiose disturbance.

○

Law and Mystery – do they co-exist? Or is Law only a requisite for masking chaos?

o

Poverty strips one of all embellishment, hence, all illusion. What a sight to see those with external comforts, internal systems and full bellies galloping on the horse of civilization – ever mushing it further without regard for the hooves that have been bleeding.

To be one without a home, a belly that aches, a thirst without wellspring – everything becomes akin to desert mirage.

The primordial dissatisfaction of sentient living-matter, the ever-present spectre of death: birth of both metaphysics and suicide.

o

Knowing that someone is involved with the process of filtering and disposing my piss, shit and toilet paper, it even becomes difficult to secrete!

o

Every street corner necessitates a Diogenes.

o

S. tells me of a sailors graveyard on the island of N., composed of anonymous headstones and a single white cross. If this body cannot be thrown to the dogs, I now know where the pinebox will be dumped.

o

Heraclitus separated concrete elements from chaos; this duality pervaded most of ancient Greek thought. A Buddhist would not separate the two – chaos and cosmos take share of the same emptiness. If cosmos was born out of chaos, how separate the two?

o

Hunger and death – the only points to stand upon. The former to maintain irrationality; the latter to prepare for quietude.

o

A man of poverty walks with torn shoes…and keeps walking.

o

For the time being, we can only *comment* on our bastard birth. Upon the moment of death, will we finally have nothing left to say? Perhaps that is the peace we vainly search for.

o

Watching a man as he shouts at an idling police car…the only conclusion for a tired State.

o

The only states that restore sense? - the nonsense of music, the nonchalance of dreams.

o

I could argue with my personal Mastema, but that would only be the denial of something *intimate*.

○

Thinking of the many that, if not for eyeglasses, would've been cut down by our brothers – a layman's way of contemplating Father Error and Mother Indifference.

○

The futility of filling our stomachs being labor enough, why bother establishing theories of the mind or participating in back-breaking work? If not for the artifice of civilization, or any of our other collective hallucinations, we would feel more comfortable in praising and aiding the bum, scamp and tramp. Men and women devoted to no cause: life is not dilated by the scope of ideas or machine-mechanics, but rather the size of the stomach. Having reduced themselves to feeding, drinking and breathing only, they reveal the rest of us as being imposters, poseurs, circus men. A man without an ascetic body? - ringmaster of the great Lie. Only the hungry ones will be blasphemous, and therefore honest.

○

Every morning I wake and stare at the ceiling, wondering just what it is that's keeping everyone from going mad; what's keeping the world from blowing itself up?... and then I remember that I have to get ready for work.

○

Nietzsche's one worthy idea was that of a monastery for non-believers.

○

Philosophy and religion: exercises in death-preparedness.

○

Expectation leeches on every transaction and exchange – a bet of variables in games of unknown certainty.

○

Because our actions, thoughts and feelings are specifically human, we can never find salvation or escape from our being; I do not know if this is imprisonment.

○

When the police begin to praise themselves for their sadism and discrimination, only then will the public rest easy – power and judgement are principles that best thrive in the open air; and no two principles are better received in the decadent West.

○

We have prodded our minds too deeply; we have bet on dreams too assuredly.

○

A time for flora and fauna to quiet down – the planet dims in wonderful Autumn.

o

If we but had the courage to gather with others as companions in suffering…over a drink at happy hour…

o

Made in United States
Troutdale, OR
08/08/2024

21842987R00020